THE TEACHINGS OF YOGI BHAJAN

Laws of Life

❧

Edited by
Hargopal Kaur Khalsa

Kundalini Research Institute
Training ❧ *Publishing* ❧ *Research* ❧ *Resources*

© 2013 Hargopal Kaur Khalsa

Published by the Kundalini Research Institute

PO Box 1819
Santa Cruz, NM 87532
www.kundaliniresearchinstitute.org

ISBN 978-1-934532-88-1

Production Editor: Sat Purkh Kaur Khalsa
Consulting Editor: Nirvair Singh Khalsa
Photography: Prabhu Jot (Melinda) Hess, Convivial Design Studios
Model: Nirvair Singh Khalsa
KRI Review: Siri Neel Kaur Khalsa
Design & Layout: PranaProjects, Ditta Khalsa & Biljana Nedelkovska

The diet, exercise and lifestyle suggestions in this book come from ancient yogic traditions. Nothing in this book should be construed as medical advice. Any recipes mentioned herein may contain potent herbs, botanicals and naturally occurring ingredients which have traditionally been used to support the structure and function of the human body. Always check with your personal physician or licensed health care practitioner before making any significant modification in your diet or lifestyle, to insure that the ingredients or lifestyle changes are appropriate for your personal health condition and consistent with any medication you may be taking. For more information about Kundalini Yoga as taught by Yogi Bhajan® please see www.yogibhajan.org and www.kundaliniresearchinstitute.org.

This publication has received the KRI Seal of Approval. This Seal is given only to products that have been reviewed for accuracy and integrity of the sections containing the 3HO lifestyle and Kundalini Yoga as taught by Yogi Bhajan®.

For Yogi Bhajan who gave and gave and gave.
And is still giving. Thank you.

Table of Contents

❧

Introduction to Yogi Bhajan   *ix*

Introduction to the Meditations   *xi*

Five Sutras for the Aquarian Age   *xiv*

The Law of Identity   *1*

Meditation for the Faculty of Self-Engagement   *6*

The Law of the Beloved   *9*

Sarab Giaan Kriya   *14*

The Law of Karma   *19*

Meditation for the Arcline and to
Clear the Karmas   *26*

The Law of Male and Female   *31*

Merger of the Sun and Moon   *38*

The Law of Communication 43
The Nature of Communication 46

The Law of Balance and Polarity 49
Eliminate Cause and Effect and
Balance the Self 58

The Laws of Life 63
Sodarshan Chakra Kriya 84

The Law of Nature 89
Cover Your Karma 94

The Law of Projectivity 97
Become a Master of the Space:
A Gutkaa Meditation 100

Laws to Live By 103
Feel God within You 108

The Law of Infinity 111
Achieve an Experience of God 118

References 121

About the Editor   *139*

Resources   *143*

Introduction to Yogi Bhajan

❧

Yogi Bhajan was a spiritual teacher, a master of Kundalini Yoga, the Mahan Tantric, and a conscious business man. For him, business was a method through which spiritual principles could be learned and lived. He had the ability to relate to anyone. He could connect with people at their own level, and uplift them. When he lectured, it was amazing how he just happened to glance at a person exactly when the wisdom he was sharing was appropriate for that individual. When I had a question, before it was even voiced, he would look at me and answer it. We were all amazed that this would happen time and time again.

Yogi Bhajan, was also known as the Siri Singh Sahib of Sikh Dharma. He was born August 26, 1929 in a part of India that later became Pakistan. He came to the West in the late 60's, initially teaching the flower children. He shared an ageless wisdom from ancient times, delivered in a penetrating voice. The yoga and meditations he taught changed lives and put people in touch with their own soul, with their own being, and with Infinity.

Most people have heard of the Law of Karma, which is commonly stated as, "As you sow, so shall you reap." Yogi Bhajan took it to another level. He talked about going beyond karma, and taught us how that can be accomplished. Three such approaches include following Dharma. He often said where there's Dharma, there is no karma. The second approach is to develop the intuition in order to know what the impact and consequences of our actions will be before we commit to them. And thirdly, to identify ourselves in each situation that could have an other-than-graceful outcome.

From the time of his arrival in North America in 1969, Yogi Bhajan showed the way to move from the Piscean point of view to the Aquarian consciousness. He taught Laws of the Universe, Laws of Relationships, Natural Laws—Laws to Live By. In a single class, Yogi Bhajan would often talk about several different topics. This little book was compiled to combine and share some of his gems about these laws. When a quote speaks to me, I often repeat it 11 times a day for 40 days. It's been amazing to see how it changes my consciousness and uplifts me. If you also are affected by reading or chanting or doing the meditations, please share with others. Part of the beauty of Yogi Bhajan's teachings is the personal experiences we have and the joy of passing them on.

Introduction to the Meditations

BEGINNING YOUR PRACTICE—TUNING-IN

The practice of Kundalini Yoga as taught by Yogi Bhajan® always begins by tuning-in. This simple practice of chanting the Adi Mantra 3-5 times, aligns your mind, your spirit and your body to become alert and assert your will so that your practice will fulfill its intention. It's a simple bowing to your Higher Self and an alignment with the teacher within. The mantra may be simple but it links you to a Golden Chain of teachers, an entire body of consciousness that guides and protects your practice: Ong Namo Guroo Dayv Namo, which means, I bow to the Infinite, I bow to the Teacher within.

HOW TO END

Another tradition within Kundalini Yoga as taught by Yogi Bhajan® is a simple blessing known as *The Long Time Sun Shine song*. Sung or simply recited at the end of your practice, it allows you to dedicate your practice to all those who've preserved and delivered these teachings so that you might have the experience of your Self. It is a simple prayer to bless yourself and others. It completes the practice and allows your entire discipline to become a prayer, in service to the good of all.

May the long time sun shine upon you
All love surround you

And the pure light within you
Guide your way on.
Sat Naam.

PRONUNCIATION GUIDE

❧

This simple guide to the vowel sounds in translite-
ration is for your convenience. Gurbani is a very
sophisticated sound system, and there are many
other guidelines regarding consonant sounds and
other rules of the language that are best conveyed
through a direct student-teacher relationship. Further
guidelines regarding pronunciation are available at
www.kundaliniresearchinstitute.org.

a	hut
aa	mom
u	put, soot
oo	pool
i	fin
ee	feet
ai	let
ay	hay, rain
r	flick tongue on upper palate

Five Sutras
for the Aquarian Age

❶ Recognize that the other person is you.

❷ There is a way through every block.

❸ When the time is on you, start, and the pressure will be off.

❹ Understand through compassion or you will misunderstand the times.

❺ Vibrate the Cosmos, the Cosmos shall clear the path.

The Law of Identity

❧

The law is: if you are you, then all things will come to you.

———•———

You be you within your God. One line! Everything will come to you! That is a Law of Nature which nobody can deny. If a woman becomes a woman within herself and dwells within God, that woman shall have no problems whatsoever. You are the creative channel of God; therefore, any distance between you and your God is called insecurity.

———•———

You must understand, the only way that you can be recognized by the international world is if you become your own identity. Just remember it is a law.

———•———

There must be an inner balance. The fundamental frequency is "I am, I am." This is the oldest law, it is the newest law, and it is the first law. "I am, I am." Beyond that, nothing is going to make you happy and nothing is going to seem very good.

---•---

You are the Kundalini in every man. You are the universe. Just be who God wants you to be. Don't be in a human body, or what you think you should be. Stop thinking. Trust in God. Move on. The universe will follow you. That's the law and that's the privilege.

---•---

The reality is, you are a puppet of God. You are a projection of God. You are a *patanter* of the *anter*. Because you have not understood *anter*, you are crazy. Neither do you know your *banter*, your projection. What is your *banter*? Who you are. What is your manufacturing plan? If you know your manufacturing plan, you know the *janter*. *Janter* means the way you have been manufactured—the process, the technology. If you know the way of your *janter*, then my dear, you must know your *tanter*. You must know your length, breadth and your knot—the fiber that connects you. That is *tanter*. Union. Yoga. If you know what connects you, then you must know *anter*, which is your essence. And once you know your *anter*, you must know your *manter* which keeps you going! The direction! And then you must know your *patanter*, your projection.

What are you talking about, "I am a doctor."

"Oh, thank you doctor." What happened to you as a human being?

"No, I am not a human being. I am a doctor."

"I am an actor." Then who's the reactor?

You are a human being! Just be a human being! When you are reacting, then human, be an actor. But all the time remain a human being, oh fool, never forget! Why? Because that is your essence, that is your *anter*. Your *tanter*, your *banter*, your *patanter*, the whole thing. You are basically a human being. Remain so. Oh creature, never forget that you are a creature. The moment you will remain a creature, the Creator will remain around you. This is the law. That is called *patanter*.

———•———

Exactly as you are subject to this specification of time and space as longitude and latitude; if you take the altitude and the attitude of altitude, then you are free. That is your personal mantra. The hypothalamus is automatic in you. If the plate is set that you can remember your identity in the face of calamity, then calamity shall disappear. That's a law. The psychiatrist can't do it. The psychologist can't do it. The doctor can't do it. The surgeon can't do it. Nothing can do it.

At that moment, in any calamity, you have a wish to identify yourself. You are called upon. If you answer correctly, you get out of it. Calamity is a *maya*. The relationship is *chaya*, shadow. Nothing is real. There is only one real thing: you—in the beginning, in the middle, in the end—and that's your identity.

Meditation for the Faculty of Self-Engagement

JUNE 30, 1997

POSTURE: Easy Sitting Pose with a straight spine.

MUDRA: Relax the elbows along the rib cage. The forearms are angled slightly higher than parallel to the ground. The right hand faces up; the left hand faces down.

EYES: Tip of the nose.

BREATH: Inhale long and deep through the nostrils, and exhale through the mouth.

COMMENTS: You have the right to balance both heaven and earth. Let the thoughts go. Don't work your brain. It's not time to work the brain. Try to deeply meditate. You can enter into your inner circle of the psyche. It will calm down your irritated nerves and your non-reality.

TIME: 11 minutes.

TO END: Inhale deeply and press your hands together. Press hard with all your force. Exhale. Inhale again. Press hard right from the shoulders. Create the pressure all the way. Put all the pressure you can. Let it go. Inhale deeply again. Very kindly squeeze your spine and all your muscles up to your head, up to C1, and relax.

The Law of the Beloved

Lord Krishna had eighteen thousand wives and his legal wife was Rukhmani. Naarad came. Rishi Naarad is the great disciple of the god Naaraayan, whose job is to go everywhere and test people who worship God. For all those who are on a devotional path, Naarad is the angel. It is a divine angel who comes and tests them all, and freaks them out. So when Lord Krishna was sitting one day in his *darbaar*, in his court, Naarad came saying, "Naaraayan, Naaraayan." Lord Krishna got up, paid his respects, made him sit and said, "Bhagwaan, why have you come?"

Naarad said, "I have a problem."

Lord Krishna asked, "What is your problem?"

He said, "I am very horny. I feel very sexual. All my life I have said, 'Naaraayan, Naaraayan,' but now I am not going to say it anymore. I need to have and I want to enjoy a woman. And I found out that in the world, at this time, you are the Lord of the Universe and also, that you have eighteen thousand. Why don't you give me one?" Naarad was very serious, but Lord Krishna was not.

Lord Krishna said, "Are you serious?"

He said, "Absolutely serious. This is the truth. I want to live with a woman, maybe for one night, but I cannot go and talk about this thing with anybody, so I want to talk to you in confidence. Keep my secret and just spare one of your wives for one night. You have eighteen thousand. It takes eighteen thousand days if you complete the cycle. So what is wrong? Give me one."

He said, "Naarad, I'll give you one, but on one condition. If you cannot have intercourse with her, you'll remain celibate the rest of your life and you'll never again go to anybody with this question." Naarad said, "Okay, fine." So, when the evening came, the lights were put out.

Lord Krishna said, "Naarad, these are eighteen thousand *mahols*, the places where my *gopis*, my wives, live. Go to any one. This is the master key. It will open every door. And whosoever is alone, you can sleep with her." Naarad took the master key, went and opened every door. He found Krishna with everybody.

So the next morning Naarad met him again at breakfast and Lord Krishna said, "Did you get what you wanted?"

He returned the key and said, "I am going to be permanently celibate the rest of my life. But Krishna, you are not eighteen thousand. Tell me the secret of this thing."

Krishna smiled, laughed, and cracked up. He said, "Naarad, I was not sleeping with anybody. I was right here! You could have slept the whole night with me. It would have been all right. It is *they*, it is *their* worship and *their* devotion, it is *their* sincerity and it is in their purity that they created me. Because the *bhagta*, the beloved, creates the lover. The lover never creates the beloved."

The Law of Love is the Law of the Beloved.

What is the Law of Love? Love more and demand less.

The Law of Love. Love gives you the power to merge from finite to Infinity. Love gives you the power to trust from nothing to everything. Love gives you the most powerful prayer between you and your Creator. Love gives you vastness as vast as there can be. Love gives you the whole, the experience and the touch with your own Infinity as beautiful as it can be. Love is that surrender. When you surrender at the lotus feet of the Master, you become the Master. When you become the Master, you surrender your Universe to the Universe. Then you become Divine. When you surrender your Divinity to the Infinity, you become Infinity. That is the Law of Love.

---•---

The theory of love and hate is a simple theory. Everybody wants to love. But when you can't keep the flow of love, it can turn into embarrassment, frustration, and finally hate. From hate it becomes vengeance, then it becomes destruction. Everything starts with love. Love is the basic law. Hate is the other side of the coin.

---•---

The act of purification is where you see the unseen of each other. Before that, who is the lover and who is the beloved? It is not established in about eighty percent of the cases, and the matter falls apart there. In the act of purification, ninety-five percent of people fall apart. It's very difficult for people because when you purify yourself with love then you have to merge. Merger of everything in the world is easy, except for two egos. The Law of Ego is that it never merges.

---•---

Sarab Giaan Kriya

OCTOBER 30, 2000

POSTURE: Sit straight in a cross-legged position.

MUDRA: Bring your hands into *Sarab Giaan Mudra* in front of the Heart Center. Interlace the fingers with the index fingers extended pointing up and thumbs crossed. For men, the right thumb crosses over the left; for women, the left thumb crosses over the right.

EYES: Closed.

MANTRA: *Har Har Har Har Gobinday.* The version by Niranjan Kaur is recommended. Chant from the navel.

> Har Har Har Har Gobinday
> Har Har Har Har Mukanday
> Har Har Har Har Udaaray
> Har Har Har Har Apaaray
> Har Har Har Har Hariang
> Har Har Har Har Kariang
> Har Har Har Har Nirnaamay
> Har Har Har Har Akaamay

TIME: 3 minutes.

TO END: Inhale deeply, hold, and listen to the mantra—the sound is still in the air. Catch it. Exhale. Repeat 2 more times. Relax.

COMMENTS: If you chant this 8-part mantra for 11 minutes, 31 minutes or 2 ½ hours, and then recollect the sound whenever you are working, talking, moving, sitting, or sleeping, this sound will be with you. It will not leave you because each word of the mantra opens up a chakra and feeds the soul, giving you the feeling of deathlessness. This meditation cuts through the organism of destruction and breaks through the cocoon of our ego.

You can do anything and everything, but if you do not have tranquility, you cannot merge in God's infinite tranquility. If your value is not your tranquility, but your ego, you cannot *be*. Without tranquility there is no reality. Without reality there is no prosperity. Without prosperity you cannot give. Without giving you are not God. Guru Naanak says, "Work hard, earn by the sweat of your brow, then give; that one knows the path."

The Law of Karma

Just remember, every action has a reaction, equal and opposite. This is Newton's Third Law of Force. In the Orient, it is called the Law of Karma. In English we say, "As you sow, so shall you reap."

——•——

There's a law—Newton's Third Law of Force or Law of Karma—every action has a reaction, equal and opposite. What is the way to get out of it? Develop your intuitiveness through your meditative mind to the point that you do not cause a cause for which you are not willing to accept the effect.

——•——

We agree that everything is in balance, and as we create, so we destroy. As we project, so we reject. As we are high, so is the low. One who does not know the bottom cannot measure the top. We also know

Newton's Third Law of Force, which is the Law of Karma. As you sow, so shall you reap. Every action has an equal and opposite reaction. Don't think that what is in religion is not in science, or that what is in science is not in religion. Don't think that what is known is not unknown and that what is unknown is not known. Simply, there is one thing missing. We do not have the clarity of intuition and consciousness. All men are equal in the light of God. Simply some can have consciousness now.

———•———

You must understand the law of karma. If you want to be catered to, you have to pay the price. And if you don't want to pay the price, you don't want to be catered to.

———•———

Whatever you have been made to believe is not true. The truth is that every minute of your life is a challenge. You win it or you lose it. That's the truth. Either you win it or you lose it. The net result of your beliefs should be your balance sheet, not what you have been told by environments, circumstances, relatives, friends, boyfriends, neighbors or anybody else. The Law of Karma is, "As you sow, so shall you reap." Therefore, be intuitive and don't sow what you don't want to reap. If you are reaping the belief that the world is destruction and pain and no good, you are also sowing it. If you stop sowing it, you will find that it won't grow. Therefore, the keynote in life is not to sow what you don't want to reap.

---•---

In us, there is a viciousness which is satisfied by hurting others. But then, we ourselves are hurt for enjoying their pain. It is a psychological truth. The law is, when you hurt somebody, you will be hurt equally. Whatever pain you sow for others, you sow for yourself, and then you have to reap it.

---•---

Man can be forgiven by God, I promise you. He can be forgiven without even a prayer. God is merciful. But Mother Nature is not merciful at all. Her law is: As you sow, so shall you reap. She is in charge of karma.

---•---

It is a Law of Karma and the karma must be joined together. The parents are the karma of the children. And the children are the karma of the parents. That's what the relationship is.

---•---

Everything is because of the Law of Karma, but you can always become yourself and be beyond the Law of Karma. The purpose of life is to go beyond the Law of Karma. That's what Dharma is about.

---•---

Applied consciousness is Dharma. Dharma has no other meaning. If your intuition, intelligence and consciousness are not put together, you don't have Dharma. It is *parma* or *karma*. *Parma* means doubt. *Karma* means action and reaction. A Gursikh never reacts. He only acts.

---•---

It's a Law of Physics, that action shall have a reaction equal and opposite. *Aavaagavan* it is called—action and reaction, in and out, karma. The Law of Karma. The Law of Karma is action and reaction for this earth. The Law of Dharma is that which has no reaction. If you just use tact, you can create everlasting impact. Nobody shall react. Then you're a winner, though you may not know anything else.

---•---

Japaa gives *tapaa*. When you repeat the Name of God, it creates a special heat, called *tapaa*. That burns the karma and gives you the Dharma. It is a simple, known law.

---•---

This universe is governed by this law: matter cannot be created and matter cannot be destroyed. That is why in yoga we say there is no use in creating miracles.…If I produce something, then I have created a loss somewhere. I have created a cause; I must face the effect.

---•---

The denial of God is the state of anger. When there is a lot to do, one does not remember this little thing: all that is with me is because God has given it to me. The most miserable state of mind is when you think you got it. No, folks, matter cannot be created; it cannot be destroyed. It can be given to you and it can be taken away from you. Is that clear?

———•———

God is an experience of giving. Let us talk giving, all right? God gives. Follow the law. God gives, you give.

———•———

The problem is this. When you sow something today, you are going to reap it after eight or nine months, or six months, or sometimes even four months. There are some seeds which you sow today that you have to reap after two years. But under the Law of Karma, the situation you sow today, you may reap after twelve years.

———•———

Whoever shall praise the Name of the Lord shall be the Lord, recognized here and hereafter. That's what Guru Gobind Singh promised. His theory is very simple. The theory of *chardee kalaa* is to praise the Lord. Then you shall be praised by God. It is a give and take. It is a simple law. Whatever you do here, that is what you're going to get. As you sow, so shall you reap. What is above, that is below.

———•———

Every action will have a reaction. You have to pay karma.

> *Karamee aapo aapanee kay nayrai kay door.*
> *Jinee naam dhiaaiaa gha-ay masakat ghaal.*
> *Naanak tay mukh ujalay kaytee chhutee naal.*

> ꙩ From Guru Naanak's Japji Sahib

You cannot escape karma. An action sequence must lead to a consequence. This is a law in which God, Himself, is bound. So cause no cause and start no sequence for which you do not want to face the result.

———•———

Action and reaction are the continuous process of the polarity of the magnetic field in which life is vibrantly vibrant and intervibrant. The intervibrant magnetic fields are alive and well. The projectivity and rejectivity of all beings of life concentrate to produce the electromagnetic field which is called life. It is the Law of Science.

———•———

Perhaps you do not know it is called: "the act of karma." Each day, one negative thought will create one negative scene tomorrow. This is why. The cycle of the earth on the axle is 24 hours. And the psycho-magnetic field and psycho-magnetic identity must classify within 24 hours. The psycho-electromagnetic field and psycho-electromagnetic identity in projection must manifest something in one year. That's the orbit on which the earth rotates around the sun. These are two laws you can't change.

Meditation for the Arcline and to Clear the Karmas

AUGUST 1, 1996

POSTURE: Sit in Easy Pose with a straight spine.

MUDRA: Relax the elbows down by the sides, and bring the forearms straight out in front of your body, palms flat and facing up. Have the palms slightly cupped, and place them a few inches above the knees.

MOVEMENT: Bring arms up, back behind the head, stretching hands and arms as far back over the shoulders as you can. Imagine you are scooping water, and throwing it through your arcline, over your shoulders, with a flick of the wrists. The movement is smooth and gracefully flows along with the lyrics and rhythm of the music.

MUSIC: *Wahe Guru, Wahe Guru, Wahe Guru, Wahe Jio* by Giani Ji. On each "Whaa-hay Guroo" as well as on the "Whaa-hay Jee-o" do one complete round, scooping up, throwing over your shoulders and come back to the starting position.

EYES: Closed.

TIME: 31 minutes.

END: Inhale, and stretch your hands back as far as possible, hands right behind your head. Posture for the inhale must be correct. Hold: 10-15 seconds. Exhale. Repeat 3 times total. Relax.

The Law of Male and Female

❧

Let me explain to you how nature sees the relationship between male and female. There is the sun. There is the moon. There is the earth. When the moon comes between the sun and the earth, a solar eclipse occurs. The male is considered to be the sun. If you prefer the earth and earthly possessions over your female, the moon, you will be eclipsed. Period. Let me put it in simple language: You can either love your dollar or you can love your woman. Choose either of the two, but you can't love both. Do you understand? It's a Law of Nature. Don't just think I am saying it. I didn't say that you will be eliminated. I said you will be eclipsed. If a woman comes between you and your ego, and she is in the center of it, you shall be eclipsed. That is the Law of Nature. Understand? All relationships which break, break because of this.

———•———

There is a situation where the earth comes between the sun and the moon. What is it? This is a lunar eclipse. Who is eliminated? Woman. So actually, in any relationship which you have or you build, the problem is the earth. When earth comes in between, one shall be eliminated. For the male, it is the sun, for the female, it is the moon.

———•———

You do not understand your problem as a male. You are born of a woman. The element, the basic elemental ingredients of you come from her earth. Therefore, in the chemistry, you do carry the woman in you. The only area where you fall in your life is when you match up the moon with the earth. Now the question is, what to do? Match up the moon with the ether. It is the Law of Continuity. You cannot give guidance to woman based on earthly law. She knows better than you. Therefore, you have one option. You can keep the balance if you can be divine. Therefore, you must establish a divine approach to go about it. Is that clear? That is the Law of Approach.

———•———

One important law to understand is the Law of Approach. You must establish your approach to any woman, if you want to come in focus. First, talk directly to your woman. Some men think that by buttering up and by going hodge-podge about things, everything will work out. This will cause you the greatest trouble. Be direct. Be a fact. Be direct, be a fact, don't give her time and space. Be exact. That is the Law of Approach.

———•———

If you take the child or your husband, expand him and reflect him, you are a successful woman. The moon reflects the sun and expands. The moon does two things, it reflects and it expands. That is the Law of Nature.

———•———

You forget one law. The sun is alive. The moon reflects. She shall reflect you. Woman shall reflect you. She can never be you. It is a Law of Nature. What she reflects of you is your subconscious. She will never reflect your conscious. The worst you can do is expect that whatever you are consciously, that is what your woman should represent. No. She is a polarity. Woman shall represent your subconscious.

———•———

Once you unite, you meet, you conceive, and you grow. Then there is a conception, a pregnancy, and it must bring a delivery. Now, if the delivery means you start abusing your husband, then there is a divorce, and the family is bifurcated. That is a simple Cosmic Law. Through the cause, whatever effect you have created, you have to grow that effect to maturity. That is the Law of Nature.

Between a male and a female, it is not just the difference in size or build or function. It is your word and her word which must amalgamate. It is the Law of Amalgamation that can carry you through. Therefore, if you live at each other, you live like dogs. If you live with each other, you can be separated. If you live for each other, that is what amalgamation is.

Men who live off a woman are always going to betray a woman. Remember that. That's the law.

Remember this law: when a man falls, an individual falls. When a woman falls, a generation falls.

Five Laws for Women. The first law is to present yourself. The second law is to be sought after. The third law is to be Infinite. Don't barter character values for earthly benefits. The fourth law is judge yourself. If you do not want anybody else, including God, to judge you, then you must judge yourself within time and space and with your integrity. The fifth law is to be the light if you seek the delightful essence of life. . . . If you have to lean on someone, then lean on God, lean on the Word of God. So the fifth law for a woman is to be the light. If you want to trust somebody, trust the language of your consciousness. Never trust any language except the language of your consciousness and you will always be delightfully happy.

------◆------

You forget one thing and it is a fundamental principle: You are the sun and everything else is a planet which moves around you. And that is the faculty of a master. You don't move. If you move, then everything will stabilize itself. You want stability. You want security. You want to be. You want to be fulfilled. There you must stay and everything else must go. This is called the Law of the Wheel. That small Peace Lagoon is called *"Gutkaa"*[1], that little thing which stops the entire mind. So long as you move, everything will stabilize itself at your cost. What a shameful way to live. What a price to pay. But if you don't move, everything will move around you. It is a law. It is the mastery which you have to give a chance.

------◆------

1 *Gutkaa* refers to the small stick in the water wheel which stops the flow and changes its speed or course.

Any woman who shall try to mold her husband through anger shall end up with a definite separation. That's a law. I'm telling you heart to heart, you can mold a man through love, but you can never mold a man through anger and confrontation. Never. They are not born to do that.

Merger of the Sun & Moon

APRIL 22, 1977

POSTURE: Sit in a comfortable meditative posture. Chin in and chest out.

MUDRA: Bring the elbows in to the sides of the body and bring the hands palm up, fingers together, with the wrists bent back and the fingertips facing out to each side, in line with the shoulders.

EYES: Tip of the nose. As you continue the meditation, the eyes should relax and may roll up.

BREATH AND MOVEMENT:

Inhale and lift the left hand and shoulder up toward the ear, keeping the hand bent back and parallel to the floor. As you inhale, you will feel that the left nostril is more active than the right. Exhale through the left nostril and lower the hand to the original position.

Inhale and lift the right hand and shoulder up. As you inhale, the right nostril is more active. Exhale through the right nostril and lower the hand to the original position.

Continue to alternate sides and alternate nostrils with a steady, evenly paced breath, not too fast, and not too slow.

TIME: 11 minutes.

TO END: Inhale and stretch the arms up, looking through the tenth gate (the Crown Chakra at the top of the head). Exhale and relax.

The Law of Communication

~

The First Law of Social Communication is whenever you meet anyone, exalt him or her. The Second is whenever you meet somebody, share with him or her the best experience of your life. The Third is, when you meet someone, offer him or her the best of your life. Fourth, do it with both heart and head. And finally, just remember, whatever you have said, it is true. Prove it. Whatever you have said is true; it can only be true if you prove it. Otherwise you are lying. That is the difference between truth and lies—a lie is a frustrated truth which is spoken to save time and space. Each human being is capable and is competent and is manufactured to live pure under all circumstances.

--·•·--

All laws are the Laws of Space and Time. Truth must stand between logic and reason, space and time. And who can speak the truth? Who has the strength of spirit? Who knows himself? It is very difficult to speak truth. And it is very difficult to listen to the truth. It is the most difficult human intelligence test.

---•---

Before speaking, the first law is: you must know why you are talking. You must know for what you are communicating. What do you want? Do you want to put somebody down, or put somebody up?

---•---

The Law of Communication is: be simple, be straight and say it with a smile.

---•---

Just understand, the Law of Life is the Law of Communication. Either you can do it in love or you can do it in hatred but both are based on communication. Just remember that. Do you understand what I am saying? When you get what you want or you give what you want, it is considered a gift. But when you don't get what you want, then you will do everything you can to get what you want. All in life is just communication: either it is in the form of love or it is in the form of hatred.

---•---

If you want growth and grace, if you want everything, you will only get it if you follow the manners of life. The first manner in life is to listen. The second manner in life is to feel the other person. The third is to discuss and dialogue. The fourth is to come to a mutual understanding. The fifth is to plan a mutual strategy, because in action you must know what is what and what happens to what and how it's going to be. That is essential. Sixth? Keep communicating. Seventh? Evaluate. Eighth? Achieve. Ninth? Exchange greetings. Tenth, be thankful. This is a law for every human being to follow. Where do you go wrong?
Student: Listening.

Yogi Bhajan: You are right! You are absolutely right.

The Nature of Communication

OCTOBER 23, 2000

POSTURE: Sit straight in a cross-legged position.

MUDRA: Relax the elbows by the sides and lift the hands to shoulder level, palms facing forward. Fold the Jupiter (index), Saturn (middle) and Sun (ring) fingers beneath the thumbs and extend the Mercury (pinkie) finger so that it points up.

EYES: Closed.

MANTRA: *Sat Naam, Sat Naam, Sat Naam Jee, Whaa-hay Guroo, Whaa-hay Guroo, Whaa-hay Guroo Jee*

Chant loudly from the Navel Point. Use the instrumental music known as *Dhuni* to establish the rhythm.

TIME: 22 minutes.

TO END: Inhale deeply, suspend the breath, and circulate the energy to every cell of your body. Exhale powerfully. Repeat once more, stretching your spine long and circulating the sound within your body. Exhale and relax.

The Law of
Balance and Polarity

The Law of Balance is that there is always balance.

The Law of the Vacuum is there can be no vacuum.
The Law of Balance is nothing can be correct without
balance.

The problem is not your success or your failure. The
problem is the Law of Equality. You don't obey that.
Humans have always refused that law. Any progres-
sion or progress must have an equal depression and
rejection. This law cannot change. It is there. Most
great people on this earth who have achieved success
in the end have gone on to fail in certain other aspects

of life. So, life balances itself that way. Some people are very rich and very effective and absolutely great. But on the other hand, you'll find them totally nuts. It's not that you are not aware of it. Even in your life, you progress on one side very effectively and lose on the other side equally effectively. There is nothing on this planet that is not in balance.

The heavens must be produced on the earth. All people must be exalted to God. The law is simple. God sends you down. You send yourself up. The matter ends. If you just remember, God has sent you down and we are going to go up, the problems of life will be solved. There is but one God and He has only one problem: He cannot sit in peace. He sends people down and people cannot sit in peace so they must go up. You must go from where you started. That is called the Law of the Circle. You started from God. You must end with God.

A giver takes exactly the same energy as a taker because in this universe the Cosmic Law is that nothing can be destroyed and nothing can be produced.

The Law of Polarity says: whoever is positive is equally negative. And that is neutrality.

The Law of Polarity is always the same—if you reach out and do hard work, you can digest anything inside.

---•---

Deliberations are the Law of Polarities. There is a power of concentration between earth and ether. When you go higher, the gravity and pull are there. Sometimes you are so afraid of the unknown, you want to fall back to the known. That is called the spiritual fall. In Kundalini Yoga, it is called *shakti pad*.

---•---

It is a natural truth, a Natural Law. Man needs woman for the Law of Polarity. If a man could not live without a woman, then he would die, and all single men would die, right? But do they die? No, they don't. The Law of Polarity is that every projection has a reaction. And man wants to neutralize every reaction. To neutralize every reaction, he needs an equal or dependable polarity, and that is his woman.

---•---

To neutralize oneself is the essential Law of Life. If you cannot stop, you cannot be in control of your life. And if you cannot be in control of your life, you are not able to know what life is.

---•---

What you project, that much you withdraw. It is the basic law.

---•---

In America, you learned the Law of Vibration in 1961. India knew it in 5,000 B.C. Life is nothing but a vibration coming from two polarities. When the positive is in excess, there is harmony. When the negative is in excess, there is chaos.

———•———

Wherever there shall be Christ, there shall be Judas. Wherever there shall be Guru Arjan, there shall be Jahangir. Wherever there shall be Guru Gobind Singh, there shall be Aurangzeb. The Law of Polarity will never change. The question is: who destroyed themselves on the way and who delivered? Those who have *Whaa-hay Guroo* with every breath of their life shall deliver themselves gracefully, triumphantly, victoriously.

———•———

Bad and good will are yours. There's nothing bad. There's nothing good. Anything good can turn bad. Any good apple can rot. And any rotten apple can become whiskey. Any whiskey can save a wound and it can also hurt so much that you can never retreat from it. There's nothing, my love, which can leave if you love. If you love, you can't leave. If you leave, you never loved. It is the Law of Polarity. It can't happen. If there's a destiny, there's no distance. If there's distance, then fool, there's no destiny. You've lost the game. You will never win it. You can't win anyway! The law is, "*Wahe Guru Ji Ki Fateh.*" Victory unto God!

Otherwise there is no victory! There is no purity! Why? *"Wahe Guru Ji Ka Khalsa."*[2] Purity belongs to God. So long as you belong to yourself, you are not pure. Fool, you are not, because you are you, and you are actually God. There's a blend between you and God. Do you want to break that blend between you and God? Do you want to break that blend and want to be you? Then there will be no purity, and there will be no victory. With victory comes purity. *"Man jeetai jag jeet."* When you have victory over your mind, you can have the world around you.

--- • ---

You must understand, sex is nothing but the sixth sense. And the sixth sense is: whatever is projected out, that message must come in. It is a law which you don't want to accept as a human being, and it is the cause of all pain. Whatever is projected out is equally rejected in. Every gain has an equal loss.

--- • ---

It is a natural phenomenon of the human psyche that when you commit to a particular action, the Universal Mind comes under your control. It is the Law of Polarity. The more you give of yourself, the more control you gain.

--- • ---

2 Traditional spellings used; to pronounce: *Whaa-hay Guroo Jee Kee Fateh* and *Whaa-hay Guroo Jee Ka Khaalsa*

Life can be everything. Remember, there's a certain law and that law is: you should not compromise *you* for anything. All of your surroundings should be made straight in relation to that *you*. But that *you* is a very compassionate, inflowing spirit—not an ego. If that *you* is ego, then you will have more enemies and less friends. If that *you* is from the flowing spirit, then you will have more friends, but hardly any less enemies. That person who will have friends will always have enemies. The Law of Polarity is that the equal reaction shall be there. Equal and opposite.

----•----

The Law of Union is that every two polarities will join. There is no possibility of not joining. The law is that every two polarities will join and create. Then, whatever is created will be destroyed. That is the law.

> *"Jo upajio so binas hai paro aaj kai kaal*
> *Naanak har gun gaa-e le chaadh sagal janjaal."*
>
> ᢙ Guru Teg Bahadur (1428)

> "Whosoever is born, he shall perish.
> Everyone shall fall, today or tomorrow.
> Naanak, sing thou the Lord's praises and lay
> aside all other entanglements."

----•----

What is above is below. What is left is right. That's the Law of Creativity. Are you the power? Are you the principle? There are two words you have to understand. If you are the power, then you are the principle. If you are the principle, then you are the power. If you subject your principle and your power to you, you shall be destroyed and you should be destroyed. But if you put your power and your principle under your consciousness, and motivate your consciousness to merge with the higher consciousness, this is called "*Gurmat*."[3] Therefore, you have to continuously work each day, each minute, each breath, to keep watch that you are on the right path. You are walking toward higher consciousness.

Religion does not constitute life, because religion is a law. Those who do not live by the law must die by the law. You have heard that very famous statement by Moses, the Law-Giver: those who do not live by the law must die by the law.

I have done humbly what I could, but I have not done all that I wanted to do. That completion has to come through you. You have a very huge work before you! You are unable to solve your own life. Don't you

---

3 *Gurmat* means the intelligence of the Guru

understand that you have to solve Guru's life and God's life? And that the planet earth has to know you? You have to walk on your own axle and your own orbit. You have to keep everything in harmony and rhythm. Isn't this the Law of the Principle of the Universe? Is there going to be something different for you?

When a gift is received and God is not thanked, it becomes fate. When a gift is received and God is not thanked, it means that it has not been presented upon an altar. Then it becomes a curse. Every happiness given to you in life, if it is not equally thanked, becomes destruction. Do you know that? What are you, humans or worms? This is called the Law of Electromagnetic Polarity. It is a scientific law.

The Law of Balance is a Law of Applied Consciousness. You can never change it. You will get one thing. You lose the other. You get a third thing. You lose the fourth. There will always be a gap. The 'Law of Gap' is that there is no gap. How can that gap be filled? Be in gratitude. Make an attitude to be in gratitude. You will find the whole Universe will come to you.

Eliminate Cause & Effect & Balance the Self

FEBRUARY 12, 2001

POSTURE: Sit straight in a cross-legged position.

MUDRA: Press the palms together in front of the Heart Center.

EYES: Closed.

MANTRA: *Sat Naam Sat Naam Sat Naam Jee, Whaa-hay Guroo Whaa-hay Guroo Whaa-hay Guroo Jee.* Chant along with the instrumental music known as *Dhuni.*

MOVEMENT: Slide the hands up and down a few inches in rhythm with the mantra. Be constant and consistent.

TIME: 11 minutes.

TO END: Inhale deeply, suspend the breath and press the hands together as tightly as you can. Stretch the spine upward. Exhale. Repeat 2 more times. On the last inhalation, move the energy from the base of the spine to the crown and back to the base 3 times. Relax.

COMMENTS: You can do this simple meditation every day. It will rip off the cause and effect of your karmas by balancing you. In the middle of the meditation you may freak out, as the rubbing of the hands kicks out your monster energy. At that time you must classify yourself and stick with it.

The Laws of Life

❧

The Law of Life is the Law of Patience.

---•---

You are the victim of your own weaknesses. Once you get into them, then you only have to get out of them. That's called the Law of Life.

---•---

The Law of Life is not what you have learned in schools, colleges, families and religions. The Law of Life is, Obey, serve, love and excel.

---•---

The Law of the Universe is: obey, serve, love, excel. And this law will never change. Religions will change. Prophets will come and go. But those souls who would like to merge in God shall obey this law.

---•---

Everyone is master of his own destiny. Those who do not know how to be commanded, do not know how to command. Temptation is the Law of *Maya* (illusion). One who can withstand it knows the Law of Life. Assess your stamina, your potential, your basic flexibility, and know where your emotions are.

---•---

The Laws of Sacred Living:

- ~ Life has a consciousness.
- ~ Love is trusting.
- ~ Service is done in silence.
- ~ The home has a welcome.
- ~ The family prays.
- ~ Children have traditions.
- ~ Parents live in grace.
- ~ Neighbors answer the call.
- ~ The nation has morals.
- ~ The country supports its people.
- ~ Individuals have ethics.
- ~ Women are pure.
- ~ Men are courageous.
- ~ Children are innocent.
- ~ Religion gives reality.
- ~ A dynasty has traditions.
- ~ The word is lived up to.
- ~ Man keeps his promise.

~ People have songs.
~ Smiles give you strength.
~ Songs give you your self, your identity.

---•---

This is a new theory you have never heard: life is like a third eye in the balance. Out of it you beam the light, and therefore you beam the life. Life doesn't mean anything at all. Therefore the law is: if your beam is scattered, your life is scattered; if your beam is focused, your life is radiant.

---•---

Our life will be happy in proportion to our capacity of honesty. That's the law. I can't change it. You can't change it.

---•---

SIMPLE LAWS

Those who judge shall be judged. Those who judge not will never meet the judge. It is a simple law.

Question: *What is the quickest way to incorporate in yourself an admirable quality you see in someone else?*

In every subjection, you will get to the object. If you do not subject yourself to something, you can never have the object. It is a simple law. You have to direct your energy to get it. If you like something, you have to work for it in order to have it. Nothing happens without meditation.

━━◆━━

You have to learn in your life the process of consistency. You have to be consistent. This fluctuation in your life does not represent you. It only represents your fluctuation. Your caliber of life is the consistency of you. Excellent consistency makes you an excellent human being. You must come through, come what may. That is the simple law of life.

━━◆━━

The simple law of life is that you can always learn, and you should learn from every situation

━━◆━━

When things go beyond you, you cannot handle it. You cannot maintain it. Therefore, don't overdo anything that you cannot maintain. When you deliver something once, then you have to deliver it all the time.

━━◆━━

Whenever you flirt, you are never alert. Remember that law.

＊—•—＊

When you stand out, you must face the slander. That is the law.

＊—•—＊

COSMIC LAWS

For us, we live by moral, ethical rules and by laws. Life does not wait for manmade laws. Life is a vibration, consciously lived or unconsciously ignored.

＊—•—＊

The Divine Cosmic Law of Respect is: when you go to a man of grace or to a great man, never go with a naked head.

＊—•—＊

The Law of the Universe is that if you are a saint, you must live as a saint and die as a saint. A person who cannot die as a saint has not lived as a saint.

＊—•—＊

The best thing is to accept the Will of God. The Will of God is what is best for all, not what is best for you. That is the only difference.

＊—•—＊

THE DIVINE SHIELD

❧

The law to cross the crisis in life is: remain within the orbit. It is called the Divine Shield. It is called *Kaar*. It is the first word of the scripture in the *Siri Guru Granth Sahib. Ek Ong Kaar*. In One's creative domain you must exist. If you exist in God's Will, there cannot be any trouble that will not be solved.

---•---

Look at the Cosmic Law. This body has an aura. That's your shield. There is nothing God has made which doesn't have a protective aura around it. And you need a protective aura. That's why we work. We work to provide ourselves with protection. Work is a worship. Accomplishment is happiness. But, in that there are higher values and lower values. Do you work for the higher values or do you work for the lower values? That is the only point of dispute.

---•---

Why do you wear white? The law is the Law of the Prism: all seven colors shall project in you and reflect in you when you wear white. When you wear all cotton, it will be totally absorbent as part of a protective layer on your body, and your aura will increase from six inches to one foot.

---•---

FAMILY AND MATURITY

✍

Wherever we are, whoever we are, we must understand that God's Will is to create a family and to inspire a family to inspire another family. We live by the Law of Seed: from seed to seed. My environments and my circumstances should be such that whosoever comes under my influence and touch must find peace and Godliness.

---•---

Good is to spread goodness. All parents who loved their children when they were young will feel very frustrated when the children grow up. Because as parents, they became the shield, not the teachers. When you're not a teacher to the child, your child shall revolt. At a certain age, your child needed a teacher, not a parent. That law you cannot change.

---•---

The Law of the Child is to listen and learn. After twenty-one, what is the Law of the Adult? To work and experience. What is the Law of the Mature Person —the wise man, the old man? To share wisdom.

---•---

The Universal Law of Prayer says that the prayer of the mother is the most powerful. Then comes the prayer of the self. Then the prayer of the beloved. And finally, the prayer of the teacher. These are four realms of prayer before which the Divine Kingdom concedes to agree. When you fall in prayer with a motherly heart, whether you are a stepmother or a real mother, or when you fall in prayer without your ego, or if there is real love, not sexual, and the beloved prays, then there is nothing which can stop it from happening. Finally, the same holds true if your spiritual teacher prays for you. When we use the word "mother" as in "mother's prayer," we refer to the consciousness of the mother, which is not limited to or necessarily true of the woman who gave birth to the being.

---•---

Parents are those who pay the rent. There are not two rules. There's one law. The same law applies to Americans, to Japanese, to Germans, and to South Africans. It is a Law of Love, a Law of Duty and a responsibility. It is answering the call of duty as parents, so that tomorrow will leave behind a part of history that can be written with golden words.

---•---

What truth is that which cannot be explained? What sun is that which cannot be seen? What candle is that which cannot eat darkness? What human is that which cannot commit? Freaking out is prostitution. When you mentally freak out, it is mental prostitution. When you physically freak out, it is physical prostitution. When your sight or your ears freak out, it is prostitution. Whenever anything leaves the nucleus, it is prostitution. And everything which prostitutes itself must be persecuted. That is the Law of Karma. All sensories, when they lose the control of the central sensory system, must be punished. That is the law. Nobody can change it. What you have to reach ultimately in life is when your senses will not be anything but sensible enough that they can masterfully project your righteous nature, your real nature. Then you have reached God. That is the only way to reach God.

---•---

Adultery actually means that God gave to the human the Law of Consciousness. A polluted consciousness is adultery.

---•---

THE FIRST LAW

∽

Learning is to listen. To listen is the first law. If you cannot listen, you cannot learn. Listening is the Law of Living. It is the Law of Learning.

---•---

THE LAW OF RULE

In the administration of life you want to rule. What is the Law of Rule? You can only accomplish this in one way. Investigate and find out what is wrong. Then correct the wrong and make it right. By reporting things that are wrong, you do not participate at all. You exaggerate the pain. And by hiding things, pretending that there is nothing wrong, you create a time bomb. Your basic faculty should be: investigate, and whatever is wrong, correct it.

Earthly Law is when you want to escape from a situation in the time and space of that moment. Divine Law is a totality. If there is a problem, confront it, face it, establish it and clear it out. Don't put it off and ignore it.

THE LAW OF GIVING

This law applies to every sphere of life. Ask people to share with you. Sharing assures people that you want to live with them. That is the beginning of a good relationship. *"Vand Chako[4]."* Share with others. Share responsibility. Share knowledge. Share goodness. Share work. Share trust. Do it without grumbling or with a painful mind. Do it with the essence of a human being. Your essential essence must not represent insecurity.

———•———

Vand chako. Share and enjoy. This is a law of a Sikh. He shares. He gives. Not that somebody should feel that he is taking. A Sikh shares. He creates a partnership in giving.

———•———

You can only win when you give. You can never win when you take.

———•———

If one tenth of your money you give, in the name of God, to the Guru—because Guru is God on earth— God shall give you one hundred percent. If one tenth of your time you give to God—the Guru on the earth —one hundred percent of your time shall be covered. If you give one tenth of your health in service to God, as the Guru, one hundred percent of your health will be all right. Whatever belongs not to you, if you can consciously give it, you will get one hundred percent back. It is a Law of Karma.

———•———

4 *Vand Chako* means share with others.

SPIRITUAL PRACTICE

In the House of Guru Ram Das, only the Law of Humility works. Those who humble themselves at this house, their generations will always live in grace. It is a Law of Polarity. Those who will serve this house, their generations will be served through all time and space.

--- • ---

He said, "Yogiji, who is this Guru Ram Das you fit in everywhere?" I said, "That is our unknown. As long as you fit him in, we will never be unfit for anything. That is a law. It is as simple as that. Life is a very simple process."

--- • ---

The Law of Language is that within eight sentences, you must dedicate your conversation to God. Read *Gurbani* in the *Siri Guru Granth Sahib*. Within eight sutras, the entire conversation, the entire message is dedicated to God. "A woman who knows this secret is guarded by God. Nay, she is served by God Almighty," said Rishi Viaasa, the most wise sage of sages.

--- • ---

The Kundalini Yogi sees the body with awakened eyes. It is a microcosm of the universe. All the laws, energies, relationships and miraculous processes are enacted within its domain. Guru Naanak emphasized the body as a temple, as a vehicle for experience. It contains all the powers that can be gained from any outside source.

---·◆·---

The higher you go, when you fall, the worse it is. It's a Law of Life that people who walk on a spiritual path will fall apart or they will make it.

---·◆·---

Cosmic Law says: when God will give somebody an extreme blessing in his own consciousness, He will bring him to the door to receive the grace to experience the consciousness. But if a person falters, there will only be a remote chance that he will ever get back to that stage.

---·◆·---

The moment we have the spirit to practice our own discipline for ourselves, we are the incarnation of God. Then you don't need anybody. Your purity and piety have come home. I am not telling you that suffering is a good thing, but suffering will not affect you. Suffering and good luck and bad luck; great and nothing great; right and wrong will always prevail. That is the rule. That is the biorhythm of the planet's psyche because every moment in life is a moment of challenge. You don't like it, but time likes it. Time has to take away your space. That is the Law of Life. I can't change that. Your space has to be taken away by time. The only thing time can do is to challenge you. God never challenges you. Time will.

---•---

Once everybody was going before a statue of a god and offering gold and jewelry. Nothing happened. But when a devotee of God brought a flower and put it there, the hand of the god moved from the statue and picked up the flower. Devotion is a very powerful thing. It is the essence of life. If you want to experience the essence of life—what it is, what it was, and what it shall be—then you have to totally and deeply understand the law of devotion.

> *Rehit piaaree mukh ko*
> *Sikh piaare naahe*
>
> ～Guru Gobind Singh, Amrit Kirtan, page1015

I love the *Rehit*, I don't love the Sikh

In *Rehit*[5], there are rules and regulations, and those are not for impressing others. The rules of *Rehit* are for myself. My *Rehit* is for myself. My *Rehit* is given to me for myself along with everybody else. Then we stand equal on that platform to practice *Rehit* with

---

5 *Rehit* is a prescribed, daily spiritual discipline.

our personality, with our ability, with our capacity, and with our spirituality.

---•---

Obedience is the first Law of Spirituality. Because when you obey the command, you obey yourself, and you command yourself to obey the command! That's how you become superior! If I say something and you have to implement that, then you have to come through. You apply yourself and practically command yourself to produce it. And that's called experience. That's called *giaan*. That's called knowledge.

---•---

You need only one thing to practice any discipline: obedience. What I have learned, I could not have learned in six hundred years of life. I learned because I was absolutely obedient. When you are very obedient, you totally obey in reverence. Then the teachings become totally within you. The Law of Learning is the Law of Obedience. Those who know how to obey, know how to command because when you obey, you experience the command, and then you can command yourself. If you do not know the obedience, you do not know how to command a situation. I command very well because I know how to obey. I am very obedient to feel in my righteousness that God is with me.

---•---

Command has a fear. Love has a service. That is the law. Everybody is afraid of that command. But that command is under love. So fear and love are not two separate things. Fear is bad when it comes from a lower identity. Fear is wonderful when it comes from a higher identity. That is why I say, be afraid of God and no one else. The power is that of fear. Love God and no one else. It is the same thing.

⋅—•—⋅

You must understand that the ego is very limiting and the ego is not infinite. So if you want everybody to know and everybody to know you, you've got to deal with Infinity. You've got to deal with obedience. The higher caliber is that the more effectively you obey, the higher your consciousness becomes. The Law of Obedience is this: as effectively as you obey a command of higher consciousness, that infinite does your consciousness become.

⋅—•—⋅

The cycle of projectivity of a teacher and student is as endless as God. Those who shall not learn and listen in this lifetime shall be born again and again. One day, they will study with the one who shall hold the teachings in his heart and remember them in his head. This is the Undying Law of God. It is the Undying Law of "*Giaan*[6]", knowledge. Knowledge sustains the

---

6 *Giaan* means knowledge or wisdom.

human race and guides us on the path of sacredness. Sometimes, we plunder sacredness to incur karma.

----•----

Our purpose in this life is to live in higher consciousness and to teach others to live in higher consciousness. But the best test to that consciousness is humility, selflessness, and sweetness. When you teach, teach with honesty, truthfulness, and straightforwardness. As a teacher, never compromise. As a man, always compromise. The teacher who compromises is an idiot. A person who does not compromise is an idiot. The teacher does not teach for himself, but for the higher consciousness. And higher consciousness will never compromise with lower consciousness. This is a straight law that has to be considered as a law. It has to be observed as a law.

Jee kee birtha hoe, gur bhai ardas kar

꙳ Guru Arjan, page 519

Whatever is the desire of your mind,
tell your Guru.

Tell your Guru the story of your soul, the story of your mind and the story of yourself. If you tell your story to your Guru, God will listen. That's the law. When you tell your story to your Guru, God will listen. Let Guru tell the story to you, too. That's why you call it *hukam*[7]. We take a *hukam* and Guru tells his story to you. Guru gives his command to you. And you tell your story to the Guru. In between, ideally, you find God listening.

⎯⎯•⎯⎯

Once a thought comes, it shall manifest. That is the Law of Thought.

⎯⎯•⎯⎯

> Question: *I'd like to know what it means that the mark is written on the forehead of only a few, but we want to liberate everyone?*

That is where the mark is marked. Commitment to the Dharma is when one marks the mark. The destiny written on the forehead changes at that moment when the commitment is true. That is why, in the past, people used to touch the feet of the Holy. Then all that was written on the forehead was changed at that moment as exactly the touch provided. It is called the Law of Meridian Change.

⎯⎯•⎯⎯

Somebody asks, "When will I be liberated?" The answer is, when you are not bound by the magnetic field of the earth. The law is that simple.

⎯⎯•⎯⎯

7 *Hukam* means command, order of the Guru.

Whosoever shall commit to the Guru, God shall commit to that person. That's the relationship.

---•---

Tantra is a science of *unison* which teaches from the *multison* to the *unison* through the longitude and latitude of the entire cosmos.

---•---

Why don't you get up in the morning and do sadhana? Clean your mind, body, soul, spirit, everything and come out positive, able to face each day bright and beautiful. This is a principle, a law. What you do around you to keep clean, if you do it to yourself, your surroundings will be cleaned by millions.

---•---

Everybody in one lifetime has one chance to serve one master. That is the law. It won't come back again. Remember, no master ever comes back again.

---•---

THE LAW OF THE SPIRITUAL TEACHER

∾

There's a Law of Destiny. A teacher doesn't become a teacher. A teacher is destined to be a teacher. And a student doesn't become a student. A student is destined to be a student. Whosoever is destined to be a student shall become a great master. That is the only law God cannot change, which shall prevail beyond the existence of the Almighty.

---•---

A teacher is one who links mentally with the teacher. Guru Ram Das is not away from us. When we mentally link with him, he comes to our aid exactly as a physical person would, but with much more grace. The Golden Link is the law of the soul connected through the mind.

---•---

The Golden Link: if you have faith in your teacher, you shall always be a teacher. You have nothing to learn. Teachers are not trained. That is the law. Teachers are born out of faith, not out of spermatozoa. The energy of teaching is not transferred through physical power. Rather, it transforms the physical power and it is transferred through the mental power of the teacher. When you mentally disconnect yourself from the teacher, you fall as a teacher.

---•---

LET THINGS COME

The law of happiness is. "Let things come to you." What comes to you will make you happy. What you go after shall make you miserable. The going after it will make you sweaty and miserable. Then, when you get it, you can't handle it.

---•---

If you are a human, learn. Then exercise for yourself your first right to be human. You want to be beautiful. To whom? How many of you are beautiful for yourself? After twenty years of my talking to you, have you become beautiful and said, "I look beautiful to myself"? Beyond yourself, there's no companion. Beyond yourself, you have no reality. Beyond yourself, you have no projection. Beyond yourself, you don't exist. It is very shocking to me that I see people sick inside. Any person who expands outside for his foundation is sick inside. It's a law which cannot be a lie. It's very true. If you are solid inside, you don't need the outside. Then there's a catch-22. When you are solid inside, the outside shall come. Because where there's a deity, there's devotion. Where there's God, there's Lakshmi. Wealth, happiness, prosperity—all this nonsense which you are running around for, cannot come by running around. Satisfaction cannot come from running around. That is the law—you cannot do anything outside which is not inside.

---•---

Sodarshan Chakra Kriya

POSTURE: Sit in an Easy Pose, with a light Jalandhar Bandh.

EYES: The eyes are fixed at the tip of the nose. This meditation is not to be done with the eyes closed.

MANTRA: *Whaa-Hay Guroo*

MUDRA & BREATH:

Block the right nostril with the right thumb. Inhale slowly and deeply through the left nostril. Suspend the breath. Mentally chant the mantra *Whaa-Hay Guroo* 16 times. Pump the Navel Point 3 times with each repetition, once on *Whaa*; once on *Hay*; and once on *Guroo*, for a total of 48 unbroken pumps.

After the 16 repetitions, unblock the right nostril. Place the right index finger (pinkie finger can also be used) to block off the left nostril, and exhale slowly and deeply through the right nostril. Continue.

TIME: 11-31 minutes. Master practitioners may extend this practice to 62 minutes, then to 2 ½ hours a day.

TO END: Inhale, hold the breath 5-10 seconds, then exhale. Stretch the arms up and shake every part of your body for 1 minute, so the energy can spread.

COMMENTS: Of all the 20 types of yoga, including Kundalini Yoga, this is the highest kriya. This meditation cuts through all darkness. It will give you a new start. It is the simplest kriya, but at the same time the hardest. It cuts through all barriers of the neurotic or psychotic inside-nature. When a person is in a very bad state, techniques imposed from the outside will not work.

The pressure has to be stimulated from within. The tragedy of life is when the subconscious releases garbage into the conscious mind. This kriya invokes the Kundalini to give you the necessary vitality and intuition to combat the negative effects of the subconscious mind. There is no time, no place, no space, and no condition attached to this mantra. Each garbage point has its own time to clear. If you are going to clean your own garbage, you must estimate and clean it as fast as you can, or as slow as you want. Start practicing slowly—the slower the better. Start with 5 minutes a day, and gradually build the time to either 31 or 62 minutes. The maximum time is 2 ½ hours a day.

The Law of Nature

❧

If you obey the law, the law shall obey in return. When you obey the Law of Mother Nature, Mother Nature shall obey you.

—•—

There is nothing in this world that you need which Mother Nature will not provide you. A man or woman of God is provided by God. It is a law.

—•—

Happiness is when you do something for others to uplift them. Then the entire Mother Nature comes to uplift you.

—•—

In your life, there are two ways: when you bend your spirit, the entire universe will bend with you and as you uplift, it will uplift your spirit; or you can betray yourself. Your caliber is based on negative and positive. It's just like a beautiful, beautiful day. It can pull this way, it can pull that way. And whatever you get on this earth is nothing. It's just like a day's food. "I am going to eat lunch." Then eat. Eat as much as you want: the Law of Diminishing Returns will apply. After a while you can't eat anything more.

····•····

A Natural Law cannot be broken. Every other law can be made and broken. But Natural Laws are made once and remain forever. Understand the nature of everything from its own base, its elementary seed, and expand on it.

····•····

A Natural Law is an unchangeable law. When you break the Natural Law, you shall go through a reaction. There are certain laws which are manmade, and by breaking those you will be punished by man. But there are some laws which are Natural Laws. If you break them, you will be very sorry for it.

····•····

Any life which is without a buffer, has to be a duffer's life. You can't live without a buffer. There cannot be anybody without an arc line. It is a Law of Nature.

····•····

According to the Law of Nature, every woman has an infinite impact on the earth. She is the universe. As long as she does not become universal, she cannot create that universal impact.

⋯•⋯

Your problem is that you think everybody is thinking the same thing as you. It is not true. Keep up and you'll be kept up. It is a Law of Nature. It can't go wrong. It is the law to which God Himself shall bow.

⋯•⋯

Normally, if you get a nail in your hand, what happens to you? You feel pain. Do you think that Jesus was in pain when they nailed his feet and hands? No, he was not. He didn't care—there was no pain. If your own son does something very insultingly crazy, it doesn't hurt you. It makes you angry. Insanity is resisted by the spirit. That's the law. Nature has made this body to immunize itself to pain when torture and insanity come to a righteous person. It is an automatic function of the glandular system.

⋯•⋯

"If your language is sweet, you can win the whole world." But please remember when you talk sweetly, also talk straightforwardly, because too much candy brings pimples. There is another very popular saying,

Aisey Kourey Na Ho Koiee Thuk De,
Aisey Mithey Na Ho Koiee Kha Ley.

"Don't be so sweet that everybody wants to take a bite out of you. Don't be so bitter that everyone spits you out."

Do you understand what I am saying? That is called the Natural Law. It's the Natural Law for you to speak with an understanding and listen with an understanding.

Cover Your Karma

APRIL 19, 2001

POSTURE: Sit straight in a cross-legged position.

MUDRA: Place both hands on your face, totally covering it. "Cover your face; cover your karma."

MANTRA: *Hamee Ham, Brahm Ham,* chant along with the music by Nirinjan Kaur.

TIME: 11 minutes.

TO END: Maintain the posture and begin long deep breathing while listening to the mantra. Continue for 3 minutes. Inhale deeply, suspend the breath and exhale. Repeat once more. Relax.

COMMENTS: The most difficult thing to believe is, *Hamee Ham Brahm Ham,* "We are we and we are God." I may teach another 100 years, but I will not be able to convince you that you are God. Sometimes you do not even believe that you are a part of God. You do not even believe that the One who rotates this earth can take care of your routine. Once you believe that you are God, Mother Nature will start working for you.

The Law of Projectivity

~

You cannot be subjected and subdued if you don't agree to be. There has to be an agreement between you and your nucleus projective psyche, in the instance of the magnetic field. It has to concentrate to bring both polarities to the same frequency. That creates an orbit of creativity in which your mind, soul and self agree, at the same frequency, to subject your projective and your elementary power. To agree that you are subjected. It is a Law of Projectivity, and it is God's science. It is true no matter what the time and space is. Without your own consent of defeat, there is nothing that can defeat you. That is the First Creative Law of Woman as a Being.

--◆--

Until you are still, you cannot project. That is the law.

--◆--

You do not know how to be calm. You do not know how to wait. The greatest art is to sit and wait and let it come. That is the power of projectivity.

---•---

When you are totally bewitched with an urge, what can you do to immediately get out of it? *Gutkaa, gutkaa, gutkaa, gutkaa.* "I am the Grace of God." That is a *gutkaa*. Start relating to yourself, and the entire world will relate to you at the same frequency. That is the law. Whatever frequency you will apply to yourself, the entire world will apply the same frequency. Otherwise your own frequency will compel the other frequency either to come to that frequency or be repelled back.

---•---

This Law of Projectivity is called the Law of Electromagnetic Creative Science in which everything is in absolute balance. Nothing can be created and nothing can be destroyed.

---•---

Become a Master of the Space: A Gutkaa Meditation

AUGUST 2, 2000

POSTURE: Sit straight in a cross-legged position.

MUDRA: Interlace your hands in Venus Lock in front of the Heart Center, elbows relaxed down.

EYES: Closed.

MANTRA:

> *Me within me is the Purity.*
> *Me within me is the Reality.*
> *Me within me is the Grace.*
> *I am the Master of the space.*

Chant in a monotone. Listen to what you are saying. Learn to live and remember this all of the time, as a projection and guideline of your life.

TIME: 11 minutes.

TO END: Inhale deep, suspend the breath, synchronize your body with that purity and piety, tighten every fiber and molecule. Exhale. Repeat once more. Deeply inhale and relax.

Laws to Live By

❧

In Kundalini Yoga, the law is that the person must be desireless and a deserving student in order to elevate himself above time and space. Then, the teacher should help him. As long as you will be subject to time and space, you will be subject to trouble and pain. Time has a pull and space has a duty. So between pull and duty, you are always wavering. But when your duty becomes beauty, you rise above time. When your duty becomes your love, you rise above space.

⎯⎯◆⎯⎯

The greatest problem is that we are very desireful; and we feel the more we desire and the more we fulfill our desires, the better we are. But actually the highest desire is to become desireless. That is the only desire which is worth anything. You must understand that when you were a child, you were innocent. You had milk from the bosom of your mother. The moment you became desirous and you started playing games, you had to hassle for everything else. The Law of Desire is to desire—to accumulate, to think, to run. The Guru says it is just like the deer who has musk right in his Navel Point. He runs and runs and runs like he's mad. Finally one day, he gets struck and he falls and breaks his neck and hits his navel and he smells the musk before death. The majority of you are running for this musk.

When we drive the car, we turn the key and say,

> *"Aad guray nameh,*
> *Jugaad guray nameh,*
> *Sat guray nameh,*
> *Siree guroo dayv-ay nameh.*
> *Wahe Guru ji ka Khalsa, Wahe Guru ji ki Fateh."*

You call it a ritual; I call it taking twenty seconds. If an accident is to happen, it has to happen at a certain time and space, at a certain longitude and latitude.

> *"Desh kaal milay taa vidhee ban jaandee hai."*

"Longitude and latitude must intersect at that time when a thing is going to happen."

That's a law. I cannot change time, but I can change space, so I delay you by twenty seconds.

---•---

What I am trying to tell you is the basic law on this earth; those who shall walk toward the sun shall leave the shadows behind; those who walk to create the shadows shall never see the sun.

---•---

This is the law: in relative creativity, the psyche of the polarity remains effective only if the protectiveness of the nucleus and the center of the life cycle is maintained in absolute balance, so that it can always shine. In simple English: a candle shall give you better light if you put glass around it so that the air it needs is controlled and the flame that shines can have protection.

---•---

When I am not reminded that I am part of this universe and this universe is part of me, I am not reminded that when I can see all, only then can I see God in all. Otherwise, I can't see God at all. Then I become "my turf" and "my territory." I become cruel. I become an animal, pouncing and guarding and attacking.

---•---

When you live with your applied experience and applied consciousness, then nature will teach you to reach the master. And your mastery of obedience and service will give you love and excellence. That's the law: obey, serve, love, excel.

So there is always a fight between reality and non-reality. Why? Why is there a fight? Why is there divorce here? Why is there fighting between people? Why are people not happy? Do you know why? There is a very simple answer: we think the earth is permanent. If we would just accept the earth as temporary, then we would have to accept whatever we do here. Our behavior would have to be absolutely decent. But we don't want to accept that. When we talk about *maya*, it does not mean money, it does not mean silken clothes or jewelry or a good car. You do not understand the word *maya*. *Maya* means when you want to attribute and contribute your total power of life, your *praanic* life, to succeed on this earth by hook or by crook. *Maya* means the temporary stay on earth becomes permanent, and the permanent stay of God becomes temporary. That is *maya*.

One thing to remember is, all things come from God and all things go to God.

Feel God within You

OCTOBER 10, 2001

POSTURE: Sit straight in a cross-legged position.

MUDRA: Clasp the hands together, right palm facing away from the body and left palm facing toward the body, in front of the Heart Center. The elbows are relaxed down.

EYES: Closed.

MANTRA: *Ang Sang Whaa-Hay Guroo.* Chant the mantra; Nirinjan Kaur's version is recommended. Pull the navel in and up with the 5 strokes of the mantra.

TIME: 11 - 31 minutes.

TO END: Deeply inhale and completely exhale. Deeply inhale, suspend the breath and stretch the spine and the hands up, maintaining the lock, exhale and relax.

COMMENTS: You will be surprised at what it does. Feel the Creator within you. In our heart is our God. He is not coming from the outside. Simply we have to feel it. That great feeling is *Ang Sang Whaa-hay Guroo.*

The Law of Infinity

The Law of Infinity is: when a part reaches to the whole and connects to the whole, the whole has to accept the part because it is the same thing.

You have to remove the blocks of your own personal insecurity. Then, the 70% of Infinity will start keeping you up, flowing in you, working in you, and giving you what you need to have. That is 100%! Twenty percent is you. Ten percent is the object you are dealing with. And 70% is the One who created you and the object. That is the law of 100%. Those who do not understand this live a lie. They will never know the truth.

Learn the word. If you learn the word, then you will speak the word. When you mean the word, the entire meanness of your life will go. If you mean what you say, meanness of life will never come. That's the Law of Infinity, that of God, granted to man.

⸺•⸺

God is Infinity. Anything which is multiplied by Infinity becomes Infinity. That's the Law of Infinity. So early in the morning, get up and multiply yourself. Take yourself and multiply yourself by Infinity.

⸺•⸺

Fear God because God is fearless. Fear the fearless. Indirectly that means to become fearless and have no fear of negativity. When we say, "Be afraid of the law," it only means obey the law. That means we can transmute our faculty of fear to gain positivity. When you fear Infinity, that means you obey the Law of Infinity. When you obey the Law of Infinity, then belittlement leaves you right there. That is the exact practical meaning of it.

⸺•⸺

When two elements meet together, a third element is formed that is called the one element. Two always make one. That's a Law of Nature. That's a Law of God. Man and woman meet to produce a child. That's the Law of One. You and I meet to create one.

⸺•⸺

The Law of the Vacuum is: there's no vacuum.

⋯⋯•⋯⋯

Law of the Vacuum is, God will fill in the vacuum.

⋯⋯•⋯⋯

And the Law of the Vacuum is, there can be no vacuum. You give. You will be fulfilled.

⋯⋯•⋯⋯

When your individual psyche wants to raise, to resurrect, then all human psyches will assist you. And not only the human psyches here, the whole universe assists. That is how the personal word becomes the healing word. It is just that one concentration that you concentrate on yourself, "I am, I am. I am healed. I have no fear. I have no past. Tomorrow shall be wonderful. God is with me. *Ang Sang Whaa-hay Guroo. Sat Naam*: 'True is my identity, my reality is Truth.' *Deg, teg, fateh*: 'My power to defend and my power to feed people is my victory always.'" These sounds are so powerful. When their permutation and combination are done, the human is exalted. When you are exalted or you are resurrected, a vacuum is created. And the Law of Vacuum is that there is no vacuum. So the entire psyche of the universe will uplift you.

⋯⋯•⋯⋯

The most important thing in your life is not you. That's pure negative ego. The most important thing in life is not "us." Because "us" can come and go. The most important thing is "Thou." Then all will come to you. If you rise, you create a vacuum. And the Law of the Vacuum is, there's no vacuum when you rise above everything. That's why they say, "Don't act. Don't react. Resurrect." If you resurrect, then all will come to you.

————•————

The Law of the Vacuum is: elevate and the wealth of the world will come and support you.

————•————

There is one law which cannot be changed by God, because it is God: the Law of Nothingness. In the *Mool Mantra,* it is called *Ajoonee Saibhang,* by Itself. God has two temperaments. One is the pure God, which is by Itself and doesn't do a thing. Then there is the active part of God, the Creator. The first one is *Paraa Paarbraham Parmaatmaa.* That is *Saibhang,* God Itself. And then there is the Creator God. That is God. All religions recognize that.

————•————

The law which God cannot change is the Law of Nothingness. What can you do to nothing? You cannot do anything to nothing. You can do nothing to nothing, because nothing is nothing. Anything which is multiplied by zero becomes zero. Everything multiplied by God becomes God. The Law of Nothingness is that there is no nothingness. It is like the Law of the Vacuum in physics. The Law of the Vacuum is that there is no vacuum.

———•———

God has no "in" which has no "out." God's out and in are alike, because God is One. His Oneness is Infinite. Whatever God creates, that God receives. That is the Law of God.

———•———

The Law of Human Life is that 'I' must transform itself into Infinity.

———•———

There is the Law of Inner Essence. This law states that there is an inner nucleus which runs this whole universe. It provides you all the jobs that you have to do and provides you all the jobs which are not to be done. This inner nucleus is very powerful. It is like a magnetic crystal which carries the entire essence of all essentials of this universe. Its magnitude is so powerful and so subtle that it is called the "Unknown." In the mystery of religion, it is called "God."

———•———

Whenever you have duality, you will be in trouble. That's the law. Nobody can change it. To have no duality and to have oneness and clarity of mind, you've got to keep your mind clean, smart and healthy. Not only your body—your mind also.

⋅—•—⋅

When you talk to yourself, you are the best. That is called meditation. When you are in control of yourself and you talk to yourself and you kick your negative talk with your positive personality, you will win! Even Almighty God, the Super Supreme Bull cannot defeat you. And that is the supremacy of a human over God. When God is always, always Almighty, the law is that this is always two-sided. God is the most impotent thing in the world because He cannot produce another God. Just remember: There is only one God. There are not two. Everything is in two, except for God. Therefore, when you rise and resurrect, your duality is gone. Your divinity takes over. You become God. That is the Law of Life.

⋅—•—⋅

Where there is no personal, mental and emotional sacrifice, there is no self. Where there is territory, there is no Infinity. Where there is discrimination, there is no unisonness. These are the rules you Khalsa have to learn. These are the laws you have to obey. If you territorialize yourself into the bondage of self, you will not have unisonness. Your privilege will not prevail.

⋅—•—⋅

Now I will give you the scientific law. When all the energy and the matter is synchronized into *shuniya*, into a point, it is Infinity. And Infinity knows no defeat. So how can you be defeated?

— • —

When you work for the Divinity, then the Divine is bound to pay, because it is Infinity. Therefore the payment must be Infinite. Those who take one opportunity to serve, infinite opportunities will serve them.

— • —

Achieve an Experience of God

AUGUST 22, 1986

POSTURE: Sit in Easy Pose.

MUDRA: Bring your hands to shoulder level, palms facing forward; the upper arms are close to the rib cage. Bring each hand into *Surya Mudra* with the

thumb and Sun (ring) finger touching. Keep the other three fingers straight.

EYES: Closed.

MANTRA: *Rakhe Rakhan Har.* Singh Kaur's version is recommended. Silently meditate.

TIME: Start with 11 minutes and work up to 31 minutes.

COMMENTS: Your hands are in *Surya Mudra* and you are meditating to a *Surya Shabad.* Close your eyes and go through the oneness. Let the *surya* or sun energy circulate.

References

The Law of Identity

© The Teachings of Yogi Bhajan. Source dates in order of the quotes:

- April 4, 1992. From student's personal notes. Not verified by KRI.
- July 4, 1994.Excerpt from *The Creative Aspect of a Woman*, page 68.
- July 5, 1984. Excerpt from *The Excellence of Woman*, page 87.
- July 8, 1980. Excerpt from *Depth, Dimension and Direction*, page 46.
- July 3, 1992. Excerpt from *The Caliber of Woman*, page 57.
- September 1, 1977.
- February 8, 1996.

The Law of the Beloved

© The Teachings of Yogi Bhajan. Source dates in order of the quotes:

- July 8, 1981. Excerpt from *The Oriental Woman*, page 34-35.
- July 31, 1981. Excerpt from *The Oriental Woman*, page 150.
- July 18, 1994. Excerpt from *The Creative Aspect of a Woman*, page 153.
- Excerpt from *The Science of Keeping Up*, Volume III, Number 1, 1996.
- July 7, 1987. Excerpt from *Authentic Relationships* DVD Series, KRI.

The Law of Karma

© The Teachings of Yogi Bhajan. Source dates in order of the quotes:

- July 18, 1984. Excerpt from *The Excellence of Woman*, page 174.
- June 28, 1983. Excerpt from *The Psychology of the Invincible Woman*, page 4.
- March 26, 1985. Excerpt from *The Power of Projection*, page 71-72.
- July 7, 1983. Excerpt from *The Psychology of the Invincible Woman*, page 103.
- July 15, 1983. Excerpt from *The Psychology of the Invincible Woman*, page 180.

- July 24, 1983. Excerpt from *The Psychology of the Invincible Woman*, page 243 and 245.
- February 13, 1985. Excerpt from *The Radiant Body*, page 117.
- July 15, 1982. Excerpt from *The Psychology of the Graceful Woman*, page 110.
- July 27, 1982. Excerpt from *The Psychology of the Graceful Woman*, page 190.
- June 25, 1989. Excerpt from *Trust, Tools and Temperament*, page 4.
- July 1, 1992. Excerpt from *The Caliber of Woman*, page 24.
- July 31, 1983. Excerpt from *The Psychology of the Invincible Woman*, page 310.
- July 19, 1977. Excerpt from *Women in Training II*, page 137.
- July 19, 1977. Excerpt from *Women in Training II*, page 161.
- May 10, 1987. Excerpt from *"The Path of the Giver."* 3ho. org.
- March 24, 1980.
- July 21, 1983. Excerpt from *The Psychology of the Invincible Woman*, page 416-417.
- April 22, 1990.
- January 8, 1985. Excerpt from *The Radiant Body*, page 22.
- January 6, 1990. Excerpt from "Security and Prosperity." *Yogibhajan.org.*

The Law of Male and Female

© The Teachings of Yogi Bhajan. Source dates in order of the quotes:

- Excerpt from *Man to Man, Volume 1*, page 4. Circa 1978.
- Excerpt from *Man to Man, Volume 1*, page 4. Circa 1978.
- Excerpt from *Man to Man*, page 12-13. Boston. 1978.
- Excerpt from *Man to Man*, page 8-9. Boston. 1978.
- July 4, 1994. Excerpt from *The Creative Aspect of a Woman*, page 71.
- Excerpt from *Man to Man*, page 10. Boston. 1978.
- May 26, 1977.
- Excerpt from *Man to Man*, page 45. Circa 1978.
- July 2, 1978. Excerpt from *Comparative, Comprehensive Communication*, page 3.
- Excerpt from *Man to Man*, page 45. Circa 1978.
- July 7, 1982. Excerpt from *The Psychology of a Graceful Woman*, page 44.
- Date or Resource for this quote is missing : NEED TO CHECK IN WITH SIRI NEEL KAUR ABOUT IT
- August 4, 1983. Excerpt from *The Psychology of the Invincible Woman*, page 342.

The Law of Communication

© The Teachings of Yogi Bhajan. Source dates in order of the quotes:

- July 22, 1982. Excerpt from *The Psychology of the Graceful Woman*, page156
- March 24, 1977.

- July 28, 1982. Excerpt from *The Psychology of the Graceful Woman*, page 198.
- July 10, 1989. Excerpt from *Trust, Tools and Temperament*, page 103.
- July 1, 1987
- June 27, 1989. Excerpt from *Trust, Tools and Temperament*, page 16.

The Law of Balance and Polarity

© The Teachings of Yogi Bhajan. Source dates in order of the quotes:

- March 26, 1985. Excerpt from *The Power of Projection*, page 78.
- February 13, 1985. Excerpt from *The Radiant Body*, page 116.
- August 17, 1995
- January 15, 1985. Excerpt from *The Radiant Body*, page 50-51.
- September 12, 1977.
- July 25, 1984. Excerpt from *The Excellence of Woman*, page 214.
- August 17, 1979. Excerpt from *Comparative, Comprehensive Communication*, page 182.
- March 24, 1977.
- July 7, 1980. Excerpt from *Depth, Dimension and Direction*, page 40.
- July 14, 1981. Excerpt from *The Oriental Woman*, page 47.

- March 26, 1985. Excerpt from *The Power of Projection*, pages 67-68.
- May 16, 1977.
- July 5, 1992. Excerpt from *The Caliber of Woman*, page 64.
- September 1, 1977.
- March 16, 1985. Excerpt from *The Power of Projection*, page 68.
- *Kundalini Quarterly Fall Equinox* 1976, page 12.
- Excerpt from *Man to Man, Compiled*, page 46. Circa 1978.
- July 1, 1983. Excerpt from *The Psychology of the Invincible Woman*, page 39.
- July 10, 1983. Excerpt from *The Psychology of the Invincible Woman*, page 125.
- April 11, 1977.
- October 8, 1989.
- March 26, 1985. Excerpt from *The Power of Projection*, page 67.
- August 30, 1991. Excerpt from "Attitude of Gratitude." *3ho.org.*

The Laws of Life

© The Teachings of Yogi Bhajan. Source dates in order of the quotes:

- July 2, 1984. Excerpt from *The Excellence of Woman*.
- July 11, 1994. Excerpt from *The Creative Aspect of a Woman*, page 109.
- May 1, 1991.
- August 23, 1987.

- June 23, 1972. Excerpt from *Transitions to a Heart Centered World : Through the Kundalini Yoga and Meditations of Yogi Bhajan.*
- July 20, 1992. Excerpt from *The Caliber of Woman*, page 184.
- August 3, 1981. Excerpt from *The Oriental Woman*, page 162.
- July 19, 1981. Excerpt from *The Oriental Woman*, page 78.

Simple Laws

© The Teachings of Yogi Bhajan. Source dates in order of the quotes:

- March 18, 1985. Excerpt from *The Power of Projection*, page 18.
- Excerpt from "Dear Yogiji – Questions and Answers about Mind and Meditation." *3ho.org.*
- July 12, 1983. Excerpt from *The Psychology of the Invincible Woman*, page 147.
- July 3, 1982. Excerpt from *The Psychology of the Graceful Woman*, page 14.
- July 11, 1983. Excerpt from The Psychology of the Invincible Woman, page 135.
- July 31, 1984. Excerpt from The Excellence of Woman, page 245.
- March 24, 1977.

Cosmic Laws

© The Teachings of Yogi Bhajan. Source dates in order of the quotes:

- August 17, 1989. Excerpt from "On Behalf of the Earth," *3ho.org.*
- July 22, 1977. Excerpt from *Women in Training II*, page 242.
- July 20, 1977. Excerpt from *Women in Training II*, page 178.

The Will of God

© The Teachings of Yogi Bhajan. Source dates in order of the quotes:

- July 21, 1987. Excerpt from *Crossing the Crossroads of Crisis,* page 122.

The Law of the Divine Shield

© The Teachings of Yogi Bhajan. Source dates in order of the quotes:

- July 21, 1987. Excerpt from *Crossing the Crossroads of Crisis*, page 123.
- August 16, 1979. Excerpt from *Comparative Comprehensive Communication*, page 174.
- August 14, 1979. Excerpt from *Comparative Comprehensive Communication*, page 158.

The Laws of Family and Maturity

© The Teachings of Yogi Bhajan. Source dates in order of the quotes:

- July 19, 1981. Excerpt from *The Oriental Woman*, page 76-77.
- June 27, 1993. Excerpt from *The Power of Woman*, page 1.
- July 20, 1977. Excerpt from *Women in Training II*, page 168.
- July 14, 1981. Excerpt from *The Oriental Woman*, page 47.
- June 29, 1989. Excerpt from Trust, *Tools and Temperament*, page 33.
- July 8, 1981. Excerpt from *The Oriental Woman*, page 34.
- April 11, 1977

The First Law

© The Teachings of Yogi Bhajan. Source dates in order of the quotes:

- July 19, 1977. Excerpt from *Women in Training II*, page 146.

The Law of Rule

© The Teachings of Yogi Bhajan. Source dates in order of the quotes:

- July 11, 1983. Excerpt from *The Psychology of the Invincible Woman*, page 135.
- Excerpt from *Man to Man*, page 20. Boston. 1978.

The Law of Giving

© The Teachings of Yogi Bhajan. Source dates in order of the quotes:

- Excerpt from *Man to Man, Compiled*, page 45. Circa 1978.
- March 26, 1985. Excerpt from *The Power of Projection*, page 78.
- May 9, 1996. From student's personal notes. Not verified by KRI.
- February 18, 1985. Excerpt from *The Radiant Body*, page 135.
- Excerpt from "Learning to Bless." *3ho.org.*

The Law of Spiritual Practice

© The Teachings of Yogi Bhajan. Source dates in order of the quotes:

- July 15, 1975. Excerpt from *Under the Blue Skies of New Mexico*, page 82.
- July 14, 1975. Excerpt from *Under the Blue Skies of New Mexico*, page 65.
- July 4, 1977. Excerpt from *Women in Training II*, page 98.
- January 1, 1996
- July 10, 1979. Excerpt from *Comparative, Comprehensive Communication*, page 53.
- July 12, 1979. Excerpt from *Comparative Comprehensive Communication*, page 81.
- June 27, 1993. Excerpt from *Power of Woman*, page 4.
- July 16, 1981. Excerpt from *The Oriental Woman*, page 61.

- June 27, 1993. Excerpt from *Power of Woman*, page 4.
- June 28, 1992. Excerpt from *The Caliber of Woman*, page 7.
- August 2, 1983. Excerpt from *The Psychology of the Invincible Woman*, page 319.
- April 16, 1986.
- July 22, 1981 Excerpt from *The Oriental Woman*, page 106.
- March 25, 1985. Excerpt from *The Power of Projection*, page 64.
- September 18, 1971. Excerpt from "Spiritual Teacher." 3ho.org.
- July 3, 1994. Excerpt from *The Creative Aspect of a Woman*, page 58.
- June 26, 1994. Excerpt from *The Creative Aspect of Woman*, page 12.
- July 10, 1978. Excerpt from *The Beaming Faculty of Woman*, page 45.
- July 23, 1978. Excerpt from *The Beaming Faculty of Woman*, page 85.
- August 4, 1983. Excerpt from *The Psychology of the Invincible Woman*, page 345.
- August 25, 1978. Excerpt from *The Beaming Faculty of Woman*, page 191.
- July 13, 1983. Excerpt from *The Psychology of the Invincible Woman*, page 158.
- August 17, 1978. Excerpt from *The Beaming Faculty of Woman*, page 127.

The Law of the Spiritual Teacher

© The Teachings of Yogi Bhajan. Source dates in order of the quotes:

- January 5, 1994.
- August 23, 1978. Excerpt from *The Beaming Faculty of Woman*, page 168.
- August 23, 1978. Excerpt from *The Beaming Faculty of Woman*, page 168.

Let Things Come

© The Teachings of Yogi Bhajan. Source dates in order of the quotes:

- March 15, 1995. From student's personal notes. Not verified by KRI.
- March 25,1990
- July 8, 1980. Excerpt from *Depth, Dimension and Direction*, page 48.

The Law of Nature

© The Teachings of Yogi Bhajan. Source dates in order of the quotes:

- July 4, 1978. Excerpt from *The Beaming Faculty of Woman*, page 13.
- August 8, 1977. Excerpt from *All Things Come From God, All Things Go To God*, page 328.
- March 8, 1999. From student's personal notes. Not verified by KRI.

- September 1, 1977.
- July 11, 1983. Excerpt from *The Psychology of the Invincible Woman*, page 134.
- July 7, 1980. Excerpt from *Depth, Dimension and Direction*, page 40.
- July 8, 1982. Excerpt from *The Psychology of the Graceful Woman*, page 57.
- July 11, 1994. Excerpt from *The Creative Aspect of a Woman*, page 106.
- December 31, 1991. *Harisingh.com*.
- July 31, 1981. Excerpt from *The Oriental Woman*, page 147.
- July 1, 1987

The Law of Projectivity

© The Teachings of Yogi Bhajan. Source dates in order of the quotes:

- June 26, 1984. Excerpt from *The Excellence of Woman*, page 15.
- August 12, 1979. Excerpt from *Comparative Comprehensive Communication*, page 145.
- January 14, 1985. Excerpt from *The Radiant Body*, page 38.
- July 27, 1982. Excerpt from *The Graceful Woman*, page 187-188.
- March 26, 1985. Excerpt from *The Power of Projection*, page 68.

Laws to Live By

© The Teachings of Yogi Bhajan. Source dates in order of the quotes:

- August 2, 1983. Excerpt from *The Psychology of the Invincible Woman*, page 318.
- July 19, 1981. Excerpt from *The Oriental Woman*, page 77.
- July 27, 1983. Excerpt from *The Psychology of the Invincible Woman*, page 275.
- August 2, 1983. Excerpt from *The Psychology of the Invincible Woman*, page 449.
- June 27, 1984. Excerpt from *The Psychology of the Invincible Woman*, page 25.
- March 24, 1977.
- June 27, 1993. Excerpt from *The Power of Woman*, page 3.
- July 15, 1994. Excerpt from *The Creative Aspect of Woman*, page 140-141.
- July 5, 1981. Excerpt from *The Oriental Woman*, page 5.
- July 19, 1977. Excerpt from *All Things Come From God and All Things Go To God*, page 161.

The Law of Infinity

© The Teachings of Yogi Bhajan. Source dates in order of the quotes:

- June 26, 1996. Excerpt from *Looking Into One's Self*, page 36.
- March 5, 1989.
- July 6, 1992. Excerpt from *The Caliber of Woman*, page 72.

- July 4, 1982. Excerpt from *The Psychology of the Graceful Woman*, page 22.
- July 3, 1978. Excerpt from *The Beaming Faculty of Woman*, page 10.
- June 25, 1987. Excerpt from "Control of the Mind." *3ho.org.*
- July 5, 1982. Excerpt from *The Psychology of the Graceful Woman*, page 33.
- September 11, 1992. From student's personal notes. Not verified by KRI.
- March 26, 1985. Excerpt from *The Power of Projection*, page 77.
- July 28, 1994. Excerpt from *The Creative Aspect of a Woman*, page 207.
- July 1, 1992. Excerpt from *The Caliber of Woman*, page 25.
- July 22, 1992. Excerpt from *The Caliber of Woman*, page 193.
- June 27, 1989. Excerpt from *Trust, Tools and Temperament*, page 15.
- June 27, 1989. Excerpt from *Trust, Tools and Temperament*, page 15.
- July 20, 1977. Excerpt from *All Things Come From God and All Things Go To God,* page 179.
- July 23, 2001
- July 13, 1978. Excerpt from *The Beaming Faculty of Woman*, page 47.
- July 4, 1982. Excerpt from *The Psychology of the Graceful Woman*, page 22.
- July 1, 1992. Excerpt from *The Caliber of Woman*, page 27.

- June 26, 1994. Excerpt from *The Creative Aspect of a Woman*, page 8.
- July 19, 1982. Excerpt from *The Psychology of the Graceful Woman*, page 138.
- July 15, 1975. Excerpt from *Under the Blue Skies of New Mexico*, page 81.

About the Editor

Hargopal Kaur Khalsa has been a student of Yogi Bhajan since the late 70s. She started by taking Kundalini Yoga classes, which after 3 months, inspired her to go to the Summer Solstice Yoga retreat held in New Mexico, the land of enchantment. It was 10 days of Kundalini Yoga, Yogi Bhajan lecturing and teaching meditations and White Tantric Yoga, and there was no turning back. You know when your soul resonates. In one of the Summer Solstice retreats Yogi Bhajan led a meditation in which hundreds of us experienced universal love. It was so profound that today, over 20 years later, my heart opens and expands just thinking of it.

Hargopal has a healing practice and teaches Sat Nam Rasayan®, an ancient yogic healing modality. She is also a facilitator of Family Constellations. These healing approaches are her passion. With a background in Physics, Hargopal has worked in the aerospace industry for over 30 years. Hargopal has built upon her early love of Physics and its pursuit of understanding reality into a passion for these pragmatic metaphysical healing approaches that combine compassion, service, self-transformation, and consciousness.

Resources

The Kundalini Research Institute
Your Source for Kundalini Yoga as Taught by Yogi Bhajan®
Teacher Training, Online Resources, Publishing, and
Research
www.kundaliniresearchinstitute.org

The Yogi Bhajan Library of Teachings
Keeping the Legacy Alive!
www.yogibhajan.org

3HO - Healthy Happy Holy Organization
For information regarding international events:
www.3HO.org

To find a teacher in your area or for more information
about becoming a Kundalini Yoga teacher:
www.kundaliniyoga.com

For more information about mantras and music used with
these meditations:
www.kundaliniresearchinstitute.org
www.spiritvoyage.com
iTunes or CDBaby.com